Why the Sky Is Far Away

Why the Sky Is Far Away

A FOLKTALE FROM NIGERIA

Retold by Mary-Joan Gerson

Illustrated by Hope Meryman

HARCOURT BRACE JOVANOVICH, INC., NEW YORK

Grateful acknowledgment is made to Ulli Beier for permission to adapt "Why the Sky Is Far Away," which appeared originally in *The Origin of Life and Death*, Heinemann, 1966.

B   C   D   E   F   G   H   I   J   K

Library of Congress Cataloging in Publication Data

Gerson, Mary-Joan.
Why the sky is far away.

SUMMARY: The sky was once so close to the Earth that people cut parts of it to eat but their waste and greed caused the sky to move far away.
[1. Folklore—Nigeria]   I. Meryman, Hope, illus.
II. Title.
PZ8.1.G354Wh   398.2'6'09669 [E]   73-17343
ISBN 0-15-296310-3

To Charles, Daniel, and Jessica
and to Nigeria

In the beginning the sky was very close to the earth. In that time men did not have to sow crops and harvest them, and women did not have to prepare soup and cook rice. Anybody who was hungry just cut a piece of the sky off and ate it. It was delicious, too. Sometimes the sky tasted like meat stew, sometimes like roasted corn, and sometimes like ripe pineapple.

There was very little work to do, and so people spent their time weaving beautiful cloth, carving handsome statues, and retelling tales of adventure.

The king of the land was called the Oba, and his court was magnificent. At the royal court there was a team of servants whose only work was to cut and shape the sky for ordinary meals and for special ceremonies.

But the sky was growing angry because people were wasteful. Most often they cut off more than they could possibly eat and threw the leftovers on the garbage heap.

"I am tired of seeing myself soured and spoiled on every garbage heap in the land," brooded the sky.

One morning at sunrise, the sky turned very dark. Thick black clouds gathered over the Oba's palace, and a great voice boomed out from above.

"Oba! Mighty one! Your people have wasted my gift. I am tired of seeing myself on heaps of garbage everywhere. I warn you. Do not waste my gift any longer, or it will no longer be yours."

The Oba, in terror, sent messengers carrying the sky's warning to every corner of the land. People were very careful, that is, until . . .

The time arrived for the greatest festival of the year—the festival that celebrated the power of the Oba himself.

The most important palace dancers performed all through the night, and the Oba himself, in ceremonial robes, danced for his subjects.

By the fifth day there was rejoicing in every home and on every street. However, no one cut off more sky than he absolutely needed to feed his guests. There was a danger that, in the gaiety of the celebration, people would forget to be careful.

Now there was a woman in this kingdom who was never satisfied. She could barely move when she wore all the weighty coral necklaces her husband had bought her, but she craved more necklaces. She had eleven children of her own, but she felt her house was empty. And most of all Adese loved to eat.

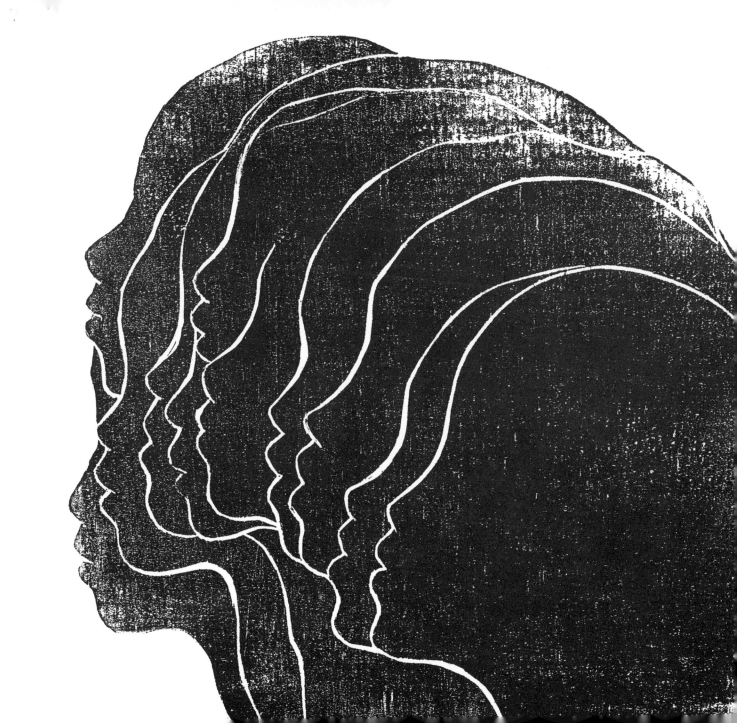

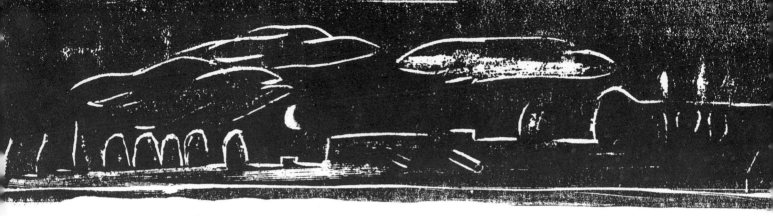

On the seventh day of the celebration, Adese and her husband were invited to the Oba's palace, where they danced and ate past midnight.

"What an evening it was," she thought later, standing in her own garden again. "How I wish I could relive tonight—the drumming I heard, the riches I saw, the food I ate!" She looked up at the sky and, as if to recapture her earlier pleasure, cut a huge piece off to eat. She had only finished one-third of it when she could swallow no more.

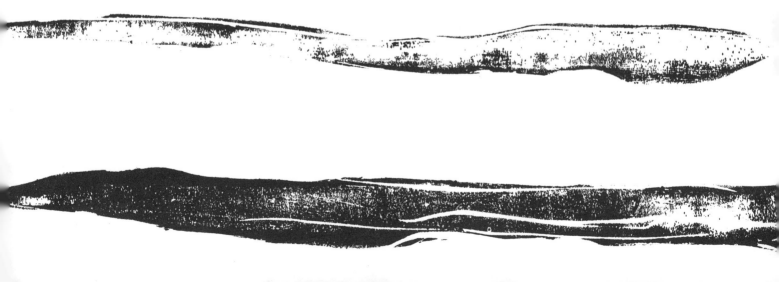

"What have I done?" wailed Adese. "I cannot throw this away. Otolo!" she screamed, calling her husband. "Come and finish this piece of sky for me." Her husband, exhausted from dancing all night and stuffed with the sky he had eaten at the Oba's palace, could take only two bites.

"Wake the children!" screamed Adese. Now the children had enjoyed a masquerade and a party after their dinner, and most of them were still too full to even nibble at their mother's piece of sky.

The neighbors were called, and the neighbors' neighbors were called, but Adese still held in her hand a big chunk of sky. "What does it matter," she said, "one more piece on the rubbish heap," and she threw the leftover in the garbage bin at the back of her house.

The ground shook with thunder. Lightning creased the sky above the Oba's palace, but no rain fell.

"Oba! Mighty one!" boomed a voice from above. "Your people have not treated me with respect. Now I will leave you and move far away. Now you must learn how to plow the land and gather crops and hunt in the forests. Perhaps through your own labor you will learn not to waste the gifts of nature."

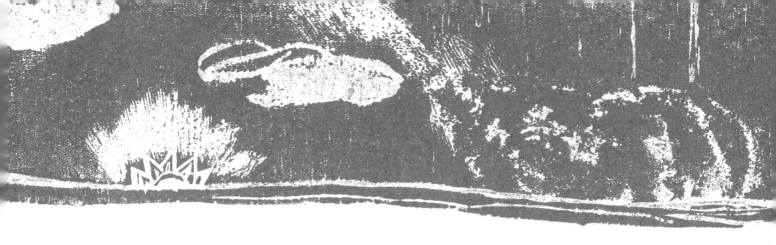

No one slept very well that night. The rising sun uncovered the heads of men and women and children peering over rooftops and through windows, straining to see if the sky had really left them. It truly had. It had sailed upward, far out of their reach.

From that day onward, men had to grow their own food.
They tilled the land and planted crops and harvested them.
And far above them rested the sky, distant and blue.

This tale was first told in Bini, the language of the Bini tribe of Nigeria, which has existed for thousands of years. About seven hundred years ago a kingship was formed in the city of Benin, and the Oba, or king, ruled the Bini people for the next four hundred years. The court of the Oba was splendid and is famous for the beautiful art created for him—carved elephant tusks eight feet long and huge plaques of bronze.

It is hard to know just when this story originated. Today there is still an Oba in Benin, but the Bini people, along with many other tribes, are part of the country of Nigeria, and today the Bini people work in factories and universities as well as on the land. But this tale is still a part of the wisdom of the Binis and one of their contributions to the culture of man.